THE WORLD'S
ENERGY
RESOURCES
Robin Kerrod

Thomson Learning
New York

First published in the United States in 1994 by
Thomson Learning, 115 Fifth Avenue, New York, NY 10003

First published in 1993 by Wayland (Publishers) Ltd.

Copyright © 1993 Wayland (Publishers) Ltd.

U.S. version copyright © 1994 Thomson Learning

Library of Congress Cataloging-in-Publication Data
Kerrod, Robin.
  Energy resources / Robin Kerrod.
        p.   cm.
  Includes bibliographical references and index.
  ISBN 1-56847-107-6 : $14.95
  1. Power resources — Juvenile literature. [1. Power resources.]
I. Title. II. Series.
TJ163.23.K46 1994
333.79 — dc20   93-34611

Designed and illustrated by Talkback International Ltd., London
Printed in Italy

Other books in the series
Food Resources
Material Resources
Mineral Resources

Cover pictures (top to bottom): Wind farm, coal mining, steel making, map of the Trans-Alaska oil pipeline.

The Maps
This book contains two kinds of maps: world maps like the one below and area maps, which show only parts of the world. The map below will help you to locate the regions shown in the area maps. Each of the red boxes on this map outlines one of the regions shown in the book. Each box also contains the number of the page on which you can find detailed information about that region.

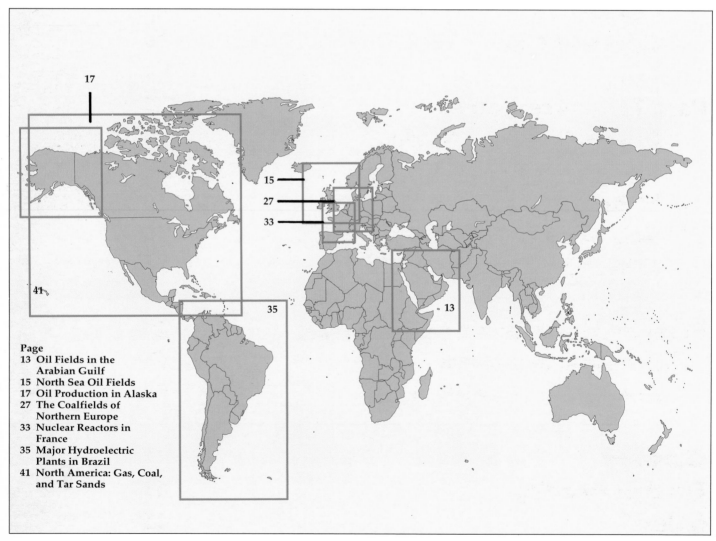

Page
13 Oil Fields in the
   Arabian Guilf
15 North Sea Oil Fields
17 Oil Production in Alaska
27 The Coalfields of
   Northern Europe
33 Nuclear Reactors in
   France
35 Major Hydroelectric
   Plants in Brazil
41 North America: Gas, Coal,
   and Tar Sands

CONTENTS

Introduction

Would your everyday life change much if you couldn't use energy? You use it when you watch television, ride in a car, or heat up a can of soup on a stove.

Television sets are powered by electricity. Electricity is a form of energy produced in a power plant by a machine called a generator. The generator is usually powered by steam. The steam is produced by heating water, using the heat energy given out by a burning fuel, most often coal.

A car is powered by the heat energy given out when gasoline burns inside the engine. Gasoline is made from crude oil, or petroleum, which we get from the ground.

The gas you use for cooking the soup also comes from the ground. If you throw away the can afterward, you are using up still more energy because energy was needed to make the can Almost everything you use, wear, or eat involves the use of energy.

Coal, oil, and gas are the world's most widely used fuels. They are called fossil fuels, because they are the remains of once-living things. The problem is that people are using up these natural resources very, very quickly.

To put off the day when fossil fuels run out, we have to make increasing use of other energy resources, such as flowing water and energy from the sun. These alternative energy resources are often called "renewable" because they will not run out.

Power from nuclear fission once promised to be the solution to our energy needs, and is today an important energy source. But the dangers of using nuclear fission have made people look for other sources. It may be that we will get our energy from improved nuclear fusion techniques — or even bioenergy, which is power from plants!

▶ Electricity is transmitted from the power plant through power lines carried by giant pylons.

PART ONE

The Fossil Fuels

The sources of energy we call fossil fuels are coal, oil, and natural gas. They are called fossil fuels because they are the decayed and altered remains of plants and animals that lived on earth hundreds of millions of years ago. Coal is the remains of huge plants that lived on land (see page 22). Oil and gas are the remains of minute organisms that once lived in the ancient seas (see page 8).

▼ Coal, in the form of coke, was first used in the iron industry in the sixteenth century. It is still used in the making of steel.

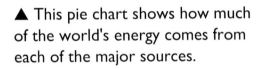

6% hydroelectric power
5% nuclear energy
38% oil
20% gas
31% coal

▲ This pie chart shows how much of the world's energy comes from each of the major sources.

People may have used coal for fuel as long as 3,000 years ago. But until the 1500s, wood was the main fuel used in the home. In furnaces used to produce metals, workers used partly burned wood called charcoal for fuel.

The first widespread use of coal was probably to heat houses in London, England. This happened in the late 1500s during the reign of Queen Elizabeth I. Coal was not widely used in industry, however, until more than a century later.

In 1709, an English ironworker named Abraham Darby invented a process for using coke as fuel in blast furnaces. Coke is made from coal in much the same way that charcoal is made from wood.

New fuels

Coal remained the most important fuel in the world until the middle of this century. But today oil and gas are more important. Together they provide more than half of the world's energy. The oil industry was born in 1859, when the American Edwin Drake drilled the world's first oil well at Titusville, Pennsylvania.

At first the main product made from crude oil was kerosene, which was used as a fuel in lamps. By the end of the century, however, demand was growing for gasoline to power the newly invented automobile.

Today there is a massive demand for gasoline. Most of the 500 million cars on the world's roads use it as fuel. Other cars and commercial vehicles use another oil product, diesel oil, in their engines. Aircraft jet engines use a special form of kerosene. These three fuels – gasoline, diesel, and kerosene – are the most important products of the oil industry.

▲ Hundreds of millions of drivers around the world depend on gasoline to fuel their cars.

Where Oil Is Found

Oil is the result of a process that began in the seas and oceans many millions of years ago, when they teemed with tiny plant and animal life called plankton. When the plankton died, they drifted down to the seabed and formed a slimy ooze, which became covered by layers of sand and mud.

Gradually, the many layers of sand and mud hardened into rock.

▲ Once oil has been found, pumps called "nodding donkeys" are used to bring it to the surface.

reached dense rock layers that it could not pass through, the oil became trapped and formed the oil deposits we find today, thousands of feet underground.

Oil fields

Deposits of oil are not found all over the world. They are found only in regions where, long ago, conditions were just right for oil to be formed.

When we find oil in a region, we call it an oil field. The largest oil fields yet to be found are in the Middle East, around the shores of the Persian Gulf. The Middle East also has the biggest oil reserves (the amount of oil in the ground)

▲ A great deal of the world's oil is found in the harsh deserts of the Middle East.

Underneath, bacteria began to break down the ooze. Heat and pressure in the earth's crust then "cooked" the ooze until it changed into the substance we know as crude oil.

Being liquid, the oil was able to seep slowly through minute holes, or pores, in some rocks. When it

World Oil Production

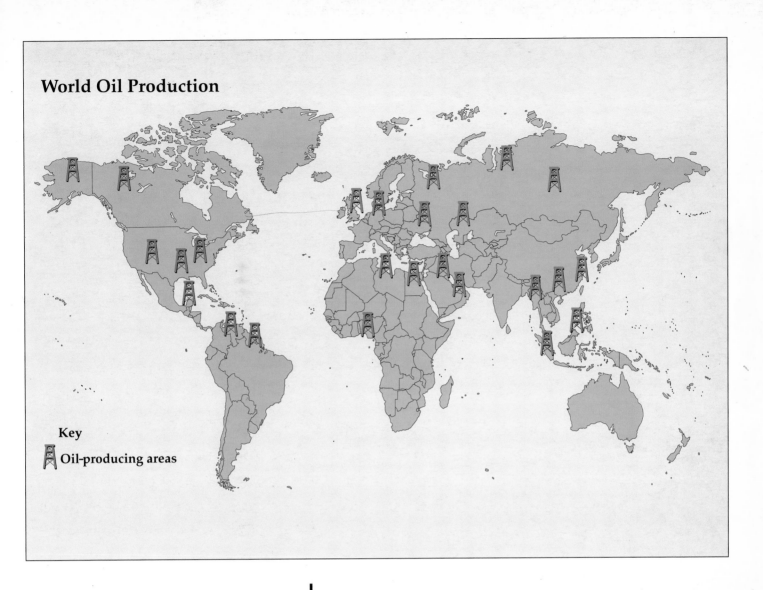

Key

🛢️ Oil-producing areas

that we know about. Saudi Arabia and Iran are the most important producers in the region.

Taken together, the countries that formerly made up the Soviet Union are the world's biggest oil producer. The main oil fields are in Siberia, in the north of the region. These countries together produce about 12 million barrels of oil a day. The barrel is the main unit in which oil is measured: 1 barrel is 170 quarts.

The United States is the second largest producer of oil, with an output of more than eight million barrels a day. Texas and Alaska are the most important oil-producing states.

In western Europe, most oil is found offshore in oil fields under the North Sea. To develop these deposits, new technologies had to be developed for drilling and production in deep water and in stormy weather (see page 14).

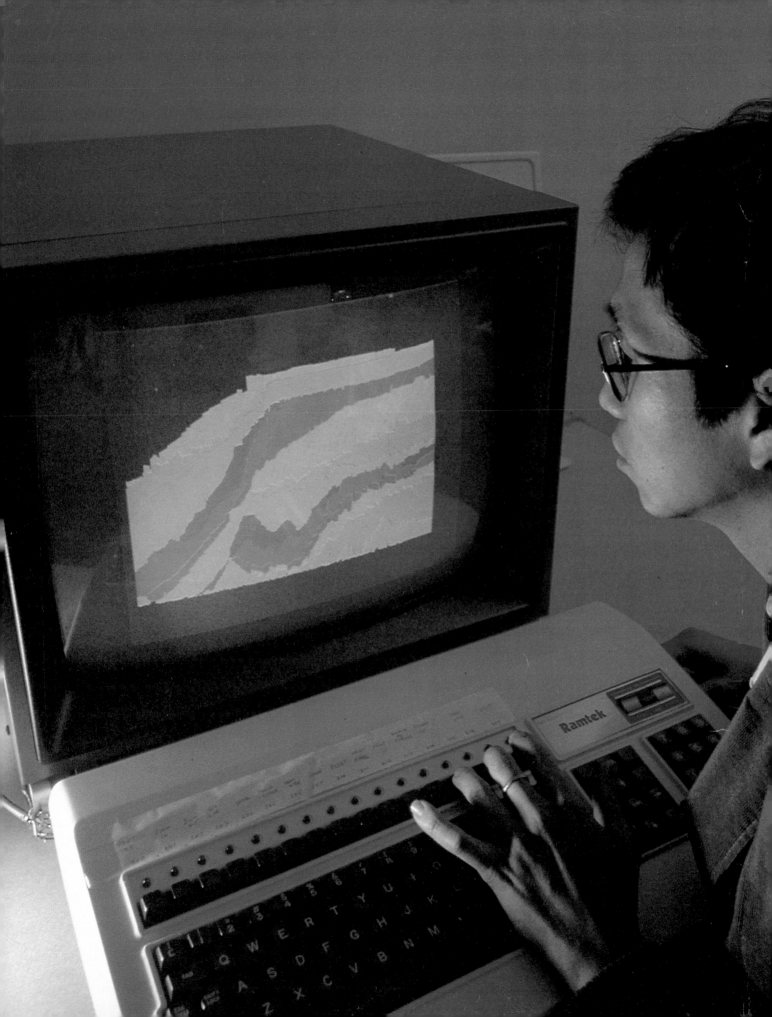

Prospecting for Oil

Oil is usually found trapped under rock many hundreds of yards underground. But there is no easy way of telling exactly where the oil is. Oil companies must do many surveys and tests before they can pinpoint possible deposits. Looking for oil, or any other valuable substance, is known as prospecting.

The people who carry out most of the work are called geologists, scientists who study the nature and makeup of the earth. First they find the kinds of rocks that they know from experience sometimes contain oil. They study geological maps, which show the different kinds of rocks, and photographs of the earth taken from aircraft and satellites. Information from these sources is also analyzed by computer.

◀ The results of a search for oil are shown on a computer. This scientist is looking at a computer picture of layers of rock underground. The different colors show different types of rocks. If the right kind of rock is found, it may mean there is oil nearby.

Rock sampling

When the geologists have found a region where the rock formations look promising, they carry out further tests. They take rock samples at the surface, and they drill deep holes to collect other samples from underground.

Geologists also take measurements with a variety of instruments, such as gravity meters and magnetometers. Gravity meters measure the local strength of the pull of gravity; magnetometers measure the local strength of the earth's magnetism. These measurements help the geologists find out what the underground rocks are like.

▲ These U.S. geologists are searching for rocks that contain oil. They are using mobile drilling equipment.

Drilling for Oil

If the geologists get good results from their tests and surveys, they can give the go-ahead for a test drilling. Oil workers then bore a hole down to where they think the oil will be. Sometimes they strike oil, and the borehole is developed into an oil well that produces crude oil. If they find no oil, the well is called a "dry well."

▼ This test drilling rig has been set up at the site of a possible oil field in New Zealand.

At least two out of every three test wells are dry.

Drilling equipment

Most oil wells are bored by rotary drills, mounted on drilling rigs, that can reach depths of 25,000 feet. The hole is bored by a rotating drill bit, which is attached to a long string of pipes called the drill stem.

The upper pipe is called the kelly. This pipe is flat-sided, so it can be gripped by the mechanism that turns the pipes, called the rotary table. As drilling proceeds and the drill stem sinks deeper into the earth, more lengths of pipe are added.

The drill pipes are hollow, and a special kind of mud is pumped down them. This flushes the rock chippings away and helps cool and lubricate the drill bit as it cuts. The mud carries rock chippings as it returns to the surface through the bored hole. By examining the chippings, the rig workers know when they are close to striking oil.

The oil in the well is often under a lot of pressure. Usually the weight of the mud in the borehole is enough to keep the oil in place.

When oil is struck, the hole can be capped and fitted with valves to control the flow of oil.

Sometimes, however, the oil rushes up the borehole and spurts high into the air like a fountain. This is known as a "gusher." It is a spectacular sight, but before the oil can be brought under control, a great deal is wasted.

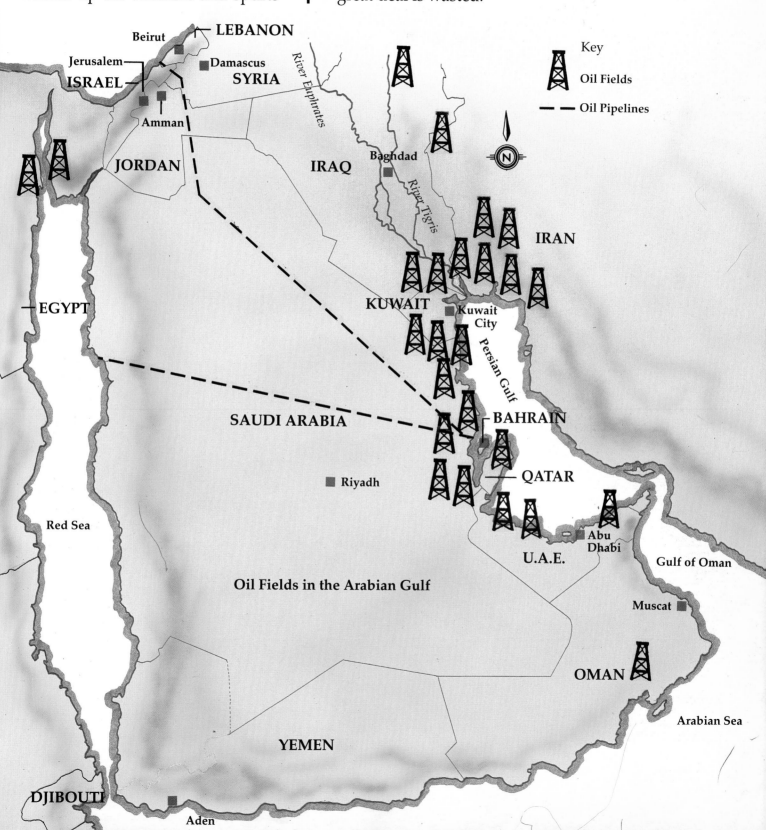

Oil Fields in the Arabian Gulf

Offshore Oil Production

Prospectors search for oil not only on land, but also offshore, on the continental shelves. These are the areas around the continents where the sea is not very deep.

▲ Offshore oil rigs in the North Sea are built to withstand the fierce storms and rough seas that are common there.

Some offshore oil fields have been worked for many years in the Persian Gulf and in Venezuela, South America. The water there is shallow and the climate is warm. More recently, oil fields have been developed in the North Sea, between Norway and England. There, the sea is much deeper and the weather is often stormy.

Drilling and production

Much offshore drilling is done by drill ships and rigs that are operated partly under water. These vessels have powerful engines to keep them in place. They drop

DIVING FOR OIL

Divers repair and check equipment on the seabed, where the water pressure is high. Ordinary divers spend a lot of time decompressing after going so deep, to make sure that they do not suffer from decompression sickness. But divers, specially trained for work under the North Sea, remain in artificial high-pressure environments for weeks at a time so that they do not have to keep decompressing.

their drill pipes down through maybe as much as 800 feet of water and then begin boring into the seabed, to a depth of one and a half miles or more.

If oil is found, a production platform is built over the well. Then new boreholes are sunk into the surrounding rocks to the oil deposit. From the production platform, the oil is loaded onto tankers or piped to the mainland.

Some production rigs are enormous. One of the biggest is the Magnus rig off the Shetland Islands to the north of Scotland. It was constructed using eight miles of steel pipe, and it weighs 15,430 tons. Over 1,000 feet high, it is taller than the Eiffel Tower in Paris.

NORWAY

Bergen

Stavanger

Sullom Voe

SHETLAND ISLANDS

Flotta

Nigg

Aberdeen

NORTH SEA

SCOTLAND

Edinburgh

DENMARK

Kærgärd

Teesside

ENGLAND

WALES

Hamburg

North Sea Oil Fields

Key

🛢 North Sea Oil Fields

— Oil Pipelines

Transporting Oil

Oil from oil fields usually has to be transported long distances to the places where it will be used. Oil is usually sent by pipeline over land, and from offshore fields to the coast. This is a very efficient method, and is cheap once the pipeline has been built.

The United States has by far the most pipelines, which have a total length of more than 18,600 miles. One of the most difficult pipelines ever constructed was the Trans-Alaska pipeline. Completed in 1977, this pipeline is 800 miles long and carries oil from Prudhoe Bay in the frozen north of Alaska to the port of Valdez farther south.

Oil is transported across the oceans in oil tankers. These are huge ships that carry the oil in

▼ The Trans-Alaska pipeline carries oil across the wilderness of Alaska.

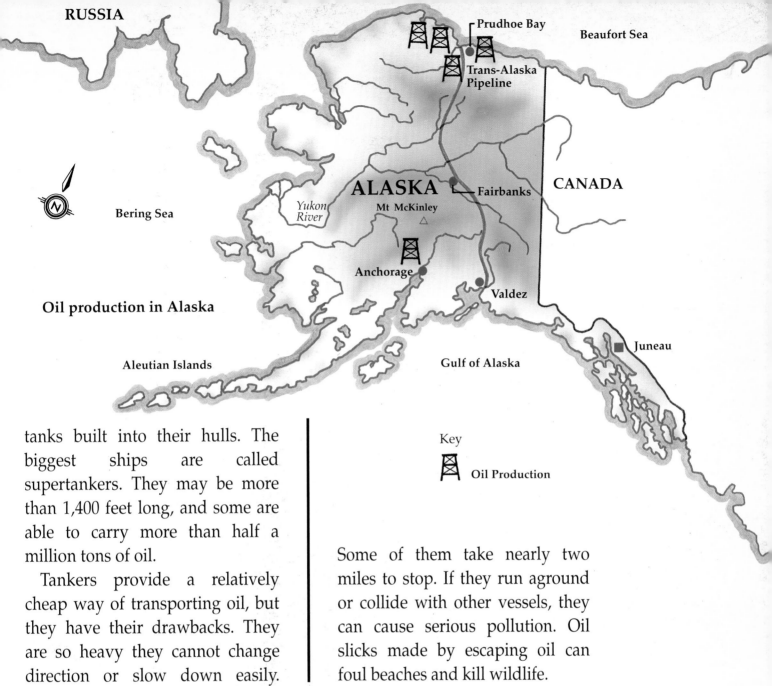

RUSSIA

Beaufort Sea

Prudhoe Bay

Trans-Alaska
Pipeline

ALASKA

CANADA

Fairbanks

Yukon
River

Mt McKinley
△

Bering Sea

Oil production in Alaska

Anchorage

Valdez

Aleutian Islands

Gulf of Alaska

Juneau

Key

Oil Production

tanks built into their hulls. The biggest ships are called supertankers. They may be more than 1,400 feet long, and some are able to carry more than half a million tons of oil.

Tankers provide a relatively cheap way of transporting oil, but they have their drawbacks. They are so heavy they cannot change direction or slow down easily.

Some of them take nearly two miles to stop. If they run aground or collide with other vessels, they can cause serious pollution. Oil slicks made by escaping oil can foul beaches and kill wildlife.

KILLER TANKER

The tanker *Exxon Valdez* ran aground in Alaska in 1989, spilling vast amounts of oil, polluting the coastline and destroying wildlife. The huge oil slick on the surface of the ocean was eventually broken up by sprayed-on chemicals and the weather. In the picture you can see the booms used to help keep oil from drifting onto the shore.

17

Refining Crude Oil

We call the oil that comes to the surface from oil wells crude oil. Another common name for it is petroleum, which means "rock oil." Crude oil is a thick, greenish-black substance. It is useful only after it has been processed at an oil refinery.

Oil is a mixture of many chemicals called hydrocarbons. They are called hydrocarbons because they are made up of the elements hydrogen and carbon.

The first stage of processing at an oil refinery is to split up the hydrocarbon mixture into different parts, or fractions. This is done by distillation (or fractionating). The oil is heated to turn it into gas. The gas enters a tall fractionating tower containing trays held at different temperatures.

The various oil fractions all condense (turn back into liquid) at different temperatures, so each tray collects just one fraction. The most useful fractions of crude oil are gasoline, kerosene, and diesel oil.

◀ Oil refineries like this one in Rotterdam, the Netherlands, turn crude oil into useful products.

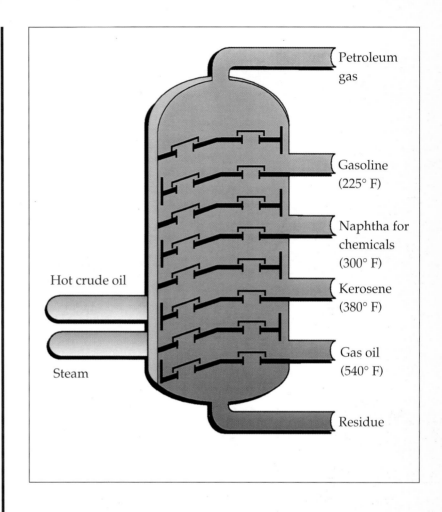

Some of the heavier oil fractions are not immediately useful, so they go to another part of the refinery for further processing, which is known as "cracking."

Cracking and other refinery processes produce a variety of useful chemicals called petrochemicals. Factories turn these petrochemicals into plastics, synthetic fibers, dyes, paints, drugs, detergents, and many other valuable products.

▲ Crude oil is separated in a fractionating tower.

Natural Gas

When oil formed in the rocks long ago, gas was also formed. Some gas is usually found trapped with oil in oil wells, but gas is also found by itself. This gas is called natural gas, to set it apart from manufactured gas, which is produced from coal (see page 26).

Like oil, gas is extracted from the ground by drilling. It is also transported in similar ways, by pipeline and tanker. In tankers, it is carried in liquid form, known as LNG – liquefied natural gas.

After oil and coal, gas is the world's most important fuel. The United States is one of the world's biggest natural gas producers.

▲ Underground caverns like this one in Lavera, France, can be used for storing gas.

GAS TO LIQUID

All gases turn to liquid when they are cooled or compressed (put under pressure). It is possible to turn natural gas into a liquid by cooling it to a temperature below -258.7° Fahrenheit. At this temperature it is stored in very strong cylindrical containers (left) or transported by tanker to the places where it is needed.

World Gas Fields

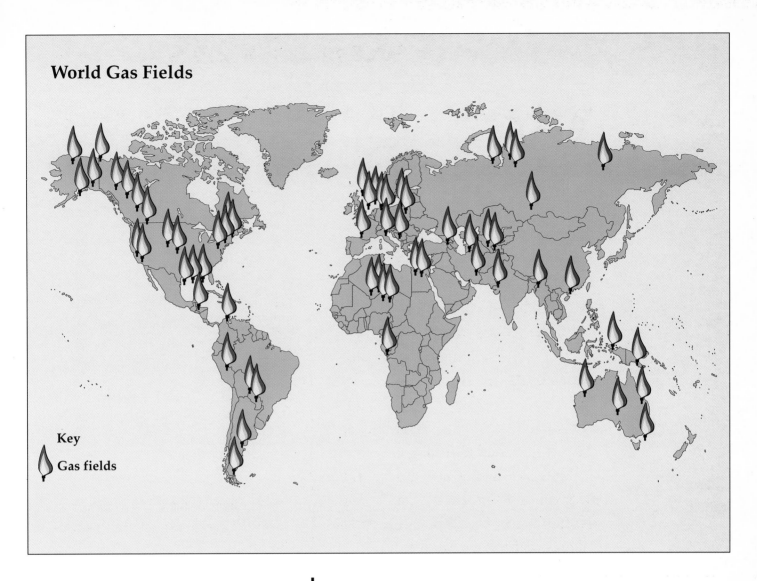

Key
Gas fields

The United States, together with the countries of the former Soviet Union, extracts over 1.7 trillion cubic yards of gas every year. Canada is also a major gas producer. The Netherlands and England take gas from giant North Sea gas fields, which were discovered and developed in the early 1960s.

Hydrocarbon gases

Like crude oil, natural gas is made up of a mixture of hydrocarbons. The main hydrocarbon is methane, the gas that is piped into our homes for cooking and heating.

The other two main gases are butane and propane. These gases easily turn into liquid when pressure is applied to them, and this is how they are separated from the methane. Butane and propane gas are sold in metal cylinders as a portable fuel supply, for example in trailers, or for household use where there is no piped gas.

Where Coal Is Found

Coal is a fossil fuel like oil and gas. About 300 million years ago tropical parts of the world were covered in swamps. In these swamps grew huge ferns and plants called horsetails, bigger than most trees living today. Eventually these plants died and began to decay, turning into peat.

Over the years, layers of peat built up and became covered by layers of mud and sand. In time, measured in millions of years, heat and pressure within the earth's crust changed the mud and sand into rock. The peat layers were changed

▼ Peat is still used as a fuel and as a soil conditioner. Here you can see it being dug up in Ireland.

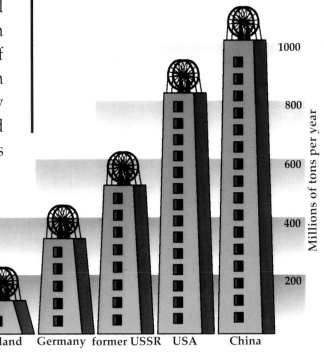

India	Poland	Germany	former USSR	USA	China

Millions of tons per year

▲ This chart shows the countries of the world that produce the most coal and the amount they produce every year.

into layers of coal called coal seams.

We call the period of the earth's history when most coal formation took place the Carboniferous Period. The word carboniferous means "carbon-bearing." Carbon is the main substance in coal.

Coalfields

Coal is quite plentiful in the world. Most coal is mined in the Northern

Hemisphere, in a broad belt that extends from North America, through western Europe, and into Russia and China.

When coal formation began millions of years ago, these regions straddled the equator. They slowly moved above it because of "continental drift" – the gradual movement of the continents across the earth's surface.

China, the U.S., and some countries of the former Soviet Union are the world's top coal-producers. China produces more than 1 billion tons a year; the U.S. produces nearly as much. These countries also have big coal reserves.

In the Southern Hemisphere, South Africa and Australia are the main coal-producing countries. It is also produced in South America by Colombia and Brazil. Coal has recently been discovered in Antarctica, but concern about damage to this special environment means that, at least for now, this coal will remain undisturbed.

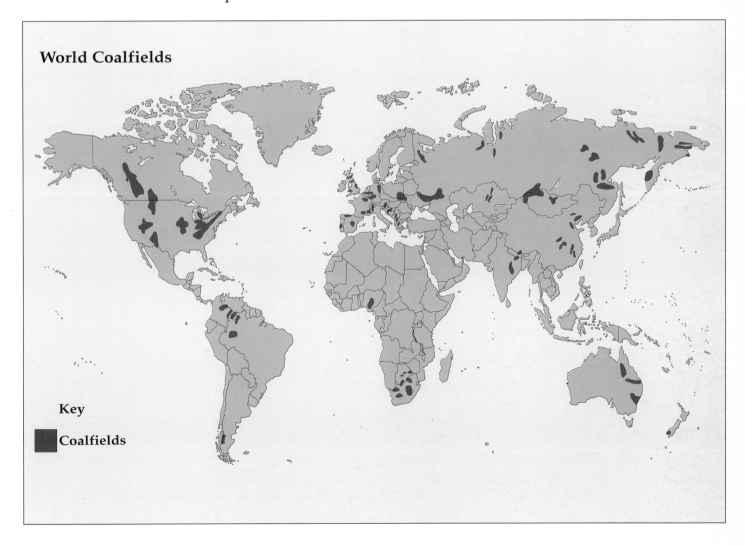

World Coalfields

Key

Coalfields

Coal Mining

Coal seams may be found close to the surface or deep underground. Seams near the surface are worked from the surface by open-pit mining. This is a simple and cheap method. Mining deep underground is much more difficult, expensive, and dangerous.

The first step in open-pit mining is to remove soil covering the coal seam. Giant excavators are used for this purpose. Some can remove 260,000 cubic yards of soil a day.

If it is hard, the exposed coal is broken up with explosives and then loaded into trucks or railroad cars. However, softer coal can be dug up by steam shovels and loaded straight from the ground.

Mining underground

In underground mining, vertical shafts are dug to the level of the coal seams. Then horizontal tunnels are cut into the seams. In the U.S. most underground mines are less than 350 feet deep, but in England coal has been worked at depths below 4,250 feet.

◀Miners working underground use powerful cutting equipment.

The place where coal is cut from the seam is called the coal face. In most mines coal is cut by machines, such as shearers. These have rotating cutting heads with sharp metal teeth.

One of the most important ways of working is "longwall mining." The cutting machine travels along a face hundreds of yards long, rapidly slicing through the coal. A conveyer takes the coal away.

Miners and machines are protected by "walking props." These are metal supports that keep the roof from caving in as the coal is cut. The props "walk" forward just a few inches at a time as cutting proceeds. Machine cutting can be highly productive. As much as 1,100 tons per hour can be produced from a single seam.

▲ Where seams of coal lie close to the surface, they are dug out by open-pit mining methods. This picture shows the Fortuna-Garsdorf mine in Germany.

Coal and Gas

▼ The impurities in coal are dumped onto huge heaps, like this one in Colorado.

Coal is not one product, but many. There are several grades of coal, which vary in the amount of heat they produce when they are burned. Coal is normally graded according to the amount of carbon it contains. Impurities such as stone and moisture are often found in coal.

The lowest grade of coal, with about 60 percent carbon, is brown coal, or lignite. It burns with a lot of smoke. The biggest open-pit coal mine in the world, the Fortuna-Garsdorf mine near Bergheim in Germany, produces lignite. The mine covers an area 3 miles long and 2.5 miles wide.

The next grade is bituminous coal, which contains about 80 percent carbon and little moisture. This was used in household fires, and it is dirty to the touch.

The best coal is called anthracite or hard coal. Anthracite is nearly pure carbon, with only traces of impurities, and is shiny and quite clean to the touch. Anthracite was produced in the earth's crust under conditions of very high pressure and temperature.

Coal into gas

Before natural gas became plentiful, the gas piped to homes was made from coal. Coal gas was used first for lighting in England about 200 years ago, and soon afterward was used widely for cooking and heating. Coal gas has now largely been replaced by natural gas.

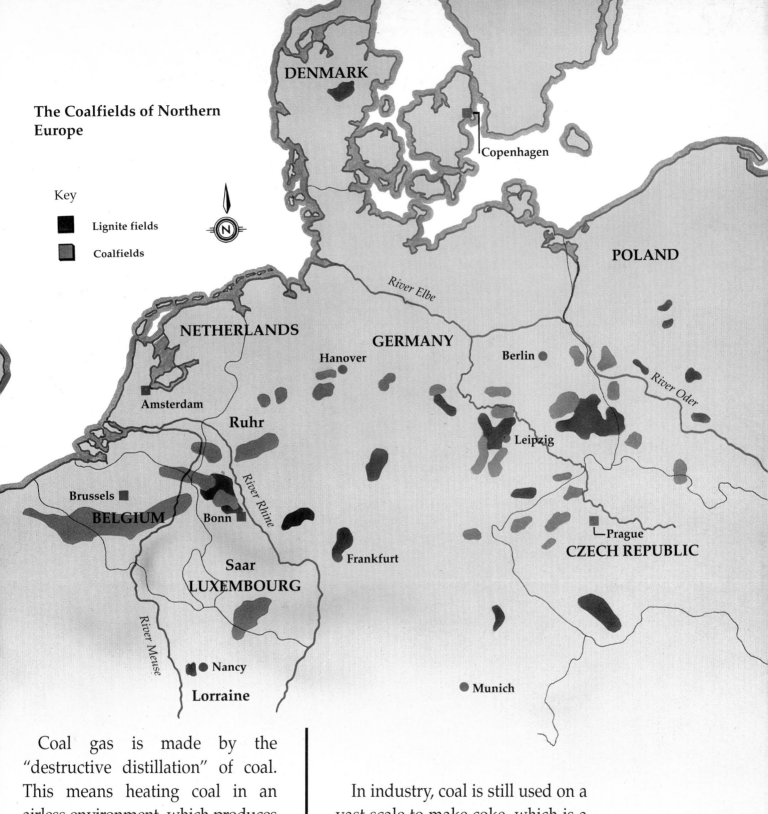

The Coalfields of Northern Europe

Key

- Lignite fields
- Coalfields

N

DENMARK

Copenhagen

POLAND

River Elbe

NETHERLANDS

GERMANY

Hanover

Berlin

Amsterdam

River Oder

Ruhr

Leipzig

River Rhine

Brussels

BELGIUM

Bonn

Prague

CZECH REPUBLIC

Saar

LUXEMBOURG

Frankfurt

River Meuse

Nancy

Munich

Lorraine

Coal gas is made by the "destructive distillation" of coal. This means heating coal in an airless environment, which produces coal gas, coal tar (a sticky liquid), and coke. Coal gas is a mixture of methane, hydrogen, and carbon monoxide and makes a good fuel.

In industry, coal is still used on a vast scale to make coke, which is a vital raw material for making iron and steel. The gas produced during coke-making is collected and used as fuel at steel works.

PART TWO

Alternatives

Fossil fuels provide nearly 90 percent of the world's energy. When they run out, we will have to rely on other sources.

At present, there are two main alternative energy sources: nuclear power and hydroelectric power. Nuclear power provides about five percent of the world's energy; the energy comes from the nucleus (center) of atoms. The first successful nuclear power plant opened in 1956 at Calder Hall in England.

Hydroelectric power uses flowing water to provide about six percent of the world's energy.

▲ The Sellafield nuclear reprocessing plant in England. This plant processes spent nuclear fuel so that it can be reused.

▶ Dams built to produce hydroelectric power from running water are spectacular sights. This one is the Glen Canyon Dam in Arizona.

Hydroelectric Power Around the World

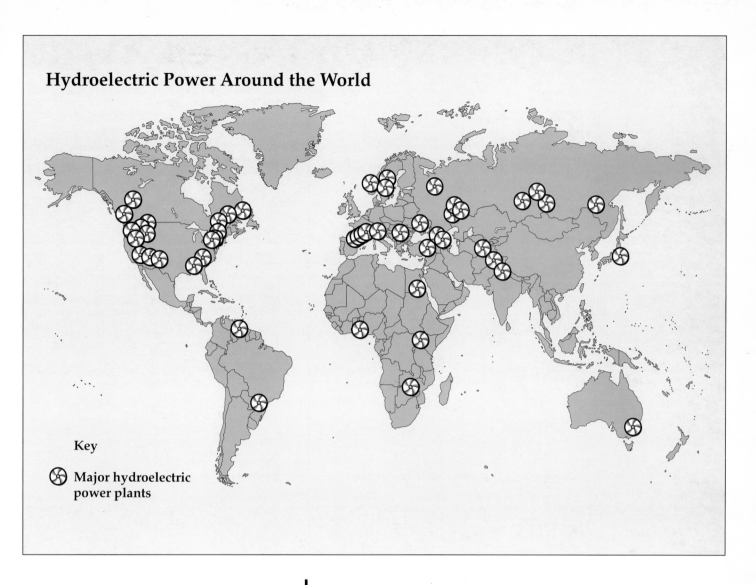

Key

⊗ Major hydroelectric power plants

The Romans harnessed this energy with the waterwheel some 2,000 years ago. The waterwheel remained the most important source of mechanical power until the steam engine was developed in the 1700s. Waterwheels were used to turn millstones for grinding grain into flour, and to power machinery. They are now used in mountainous countries, such as Nepal, to generate electricity on a small scale.

Hydroelectricity is a renewable resource. We can extract the energy in running water as long as rivers continue to flow. Energy from the sun (known as solar energy) is another renewable resource that we are just beginning to use on a large scale. The energy in the wind and the heat locked in underground rocks (known as geothermal energy) are also available as sources of energy.

Power from the Nucleus

All matter is made from combinations of pure substances called chemical elements. Each element is made up of tiny particles called atoms. Locked in the nucleus (center) of every atom is a tremendous amount of energy.

◀ This machine inserts and removes uranium fuel in the reactor.

Uranium is an element with an unstable nucleus that can be made to split. When splitting, or fission, of the nucleus takes place, a lot of the locked-in energy is released. For this reason, uranium can be used as a nuclear fuel.

The chain reaction

A uranium nucleus splits when it captures a particle called a neutron. During the splitting process, two or three more neutrons are released, along with a lot of energy. Each of these neutrons may then go on to split more uranium nuclei, releasing still more neutrons and still more energy. In turn all these new neutrons will go on to split even more nuclei, and release even more energy.

This process is called a chain reaction, and it takes place incredibly quickly, giving out enormous amounts of energy. If we do not control the process, the uranium explodes. This is what happens in an atomic bomb.

If we control the chain reaction, we can release the energy a little at a time. This is what happens in a nuclear power plant.

NUCLEAR WASTE

Nuclear power is very efficient. The uranium fuel used in nuclear power plants produces about 25,000 times as much energy as the same amount of coal. However, nuclear power has a major drawback. The waste products from the nuclear fission process are radioactive. This means that they give off radiation, which can harm living things (see page 44). Therefore, nuclear waste must be stored in special containers (right) to make sure that the radiation does not escape into the environment. Disposing of nuclear waste can be very expensive and dangerous.

Nuclear Power Around the World

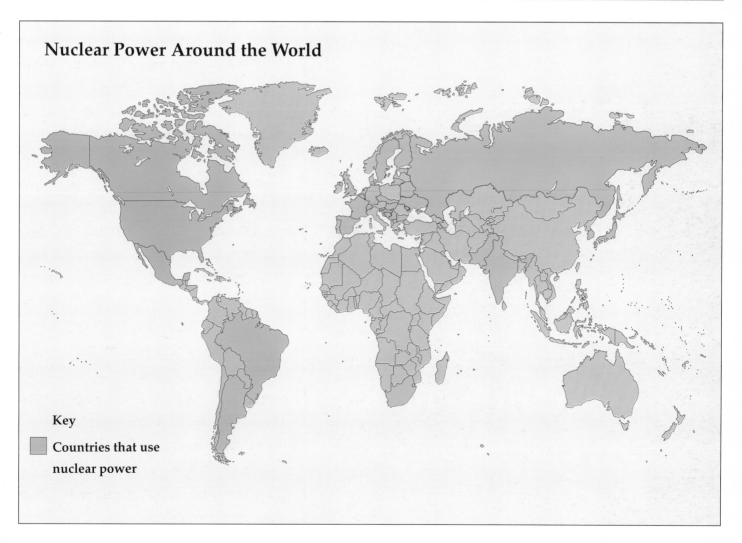

Key

Countries that use nuclear power

Nuclear Power Plants

▼ Fuel rods containing uranium must be handled very carefully. This worker is preparing to reload the reactor with fuel.

Throughout the world, more than 400 power plants in more than 25 countries use nuclear energy to produce electricity. The United States, the countries of the former Soviet Union, France, and England are among the leading nuclear-power users. France produces the highest proportion of its electricity (80 percent) by nuclear power.

The heart of a nuclear power plant is the reactor. Inside the core of the reactor, atoms of uranium fuel release their energy as heat when they split.

The heat is carried away from the core by a cooling substance, or coolant. The heated coolant then circulates through a steam generator, where it boils water into steam. The steam is then piped to steam turbines, which drive generators.

The fission process is carefully controlled to prevent the reactor core from getting too cold or too hot. This is done by means of control rods. They are raised to speed up fission and increase heat output, and lowered to slow down fission and reduce heat output. In an emergency the fuel rods drop all the way down to stop the reactor.

Reactor types

Several types of nuclear reactors are used today. The most common type is the pressurized water reactor, which uses water under pressure as a coolant. This allows for a compact design, which has led to its being used in submarines as well as power plants. Other reactors, such as England's Magnox and advanced gas-cooled reactor, use carbon dioxide gas as a coolant.

One kind of nuclear reactor, the fast reactor, uses liquid sodium as a coolant. This type is also called a breeder reactor, because it produces more nuclear fuel than it uses. Great Britain pioneered fast-reactor research at Dounreay in Scotland. France operated the first commercial fast reactor, called the Super Phenix, at Creys-Malville.

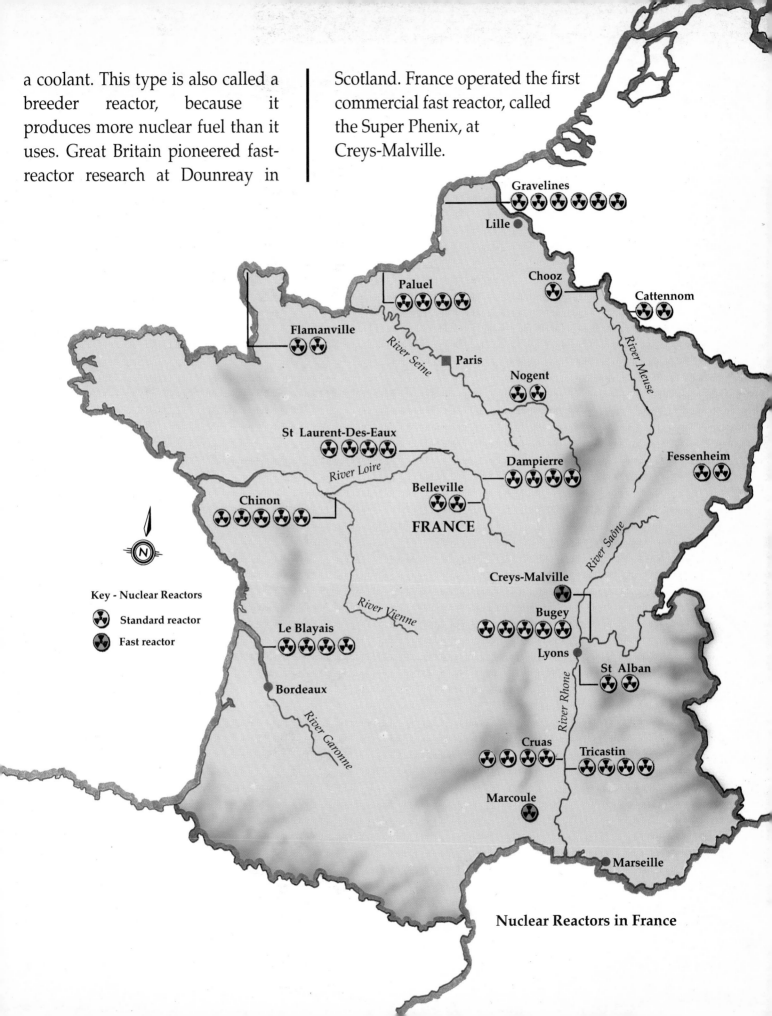

Gravelines

Lille

Chooz

Cattennom

Paluel

Flamanville

River Seine

Paris

Nogent

River Meuse

Fessenheim

St Laurent-Des-Eaux

River Loire

Dampierre

Chinon

Belleville

FRANCE

River Saône

Creys-Malville

Bugey

N

Key - Nuclear Reactors

Standard reactor

Fast reactor

River Vienne

Lyons

St Alban

River Rhône

Le Blayais

Bordeaux

River Garonne

Cruas

Tricastin

Marcoule

Marseille

Nuclear Reactors in France

Hydroelectric Power

Hydroelectric power (HEP) plants provide only about six percent of the world's energy, but they account for more than 25 percent of electricity production. In some mountainous countries, such as Norway and Switzerland, almost all the electricity is produced by water power.

The biggest power plants in the world are hydroelectric. The Grand Coulee plant in Washington State generates more than 7,000 megawatts of electric power. This is about twice the output of a large fuel-burning power plant. When fully operational, the Itaipu HEP plant on the border between Brazil and Paraguay in South America will generate nearly 14,000 megawatts.

Electricity from water

Because water flows only from a high to a low level, there has to be a difference in water level, or a "head," at an HEP plant. Usually the head is produced artificially by building a dam across a river.

The water collects behind the dam to form a reservoir. A tunnel carries the stored water into a powerhouse at the base of the dam. In the powerhouse the water is fed to a number of water turbines. These are modern versions of the waterwheel. The turbines are connected to generators, which produce electricity.

Three main types of water turbines are used in HEP plants. One is the Pelton wheel, which is designed to act like a waterwheel.

TIDAL POWER

Some HEP plants harness a different kind of water power – the power of the tides. The most successful tidal-power plant in the world is on the estuary of the Rance River in northwest France. It uses the difference in water levels between the tides to drive its powerful water turbines. The Rance River tidal barrage has been in operation since 1966.

It has cup-shaped buckets arranged around its edge, and it spins when jets of water are directed onto them.

The other main kinds of turbines are the Kaplan and the Francis. They look like ships' propellers and are completely immersed in the flowing water.

◀ The control room of this HEP plant in Tasmania, an island off Australia, is buried 600 feet underground.

Major Hydroelectric Plants in Brazil

Key

▬ Existing hydroelectric dams
▬ Planned hydroelectric dams

VENEZUELA

GUYANA

SURINAM

FRENCH GUIANA

ECUADOR

COLOMBIA

Amazon River

Macapá

ATLANTIC OCEAN

Negro R.

Branco R.

Obidos

Belém

Amazon R.

Manaus

Tapajós R.

Santarém

PERU

Madeira R.

Xingu R.

Araguaia R.

Tocantins R.

BRAZIL

PACIFIC OCEAN

Cuibá

Brasilia

BOLIVIA

PARAGUAY

CHILE

Paraná R.

N

ARGENTINA

URUGUAY

Solar Power

By far the best renewable source of energy available is the sun, which will continue pouring out energy for at least another four or five billion years.

The sun pours onto the earth about 25,000 times more energy than we need. The problem is that this energy is spread out over the earth's surface and has to be collected to produce useful amounts. Collecting solar energy is difficult, but we have made a good start.

▲ These solar cells are being used in India to power a pump that raises water from a deep well.

▼ This field of mirrors in the U.S. reflects the sun's heat toward a central water heater.

Almost all space satellites are now powered by solar energy. They are fitted with panels of solar cells, which are devices similar to silicon chips. Solar cells convert the energy in sunlight into electricity. At present, solar cells are too expensive for widespread use, although they are becoming cheaper all the time. They are used in some remote locations where other sources of power are difficult to get.

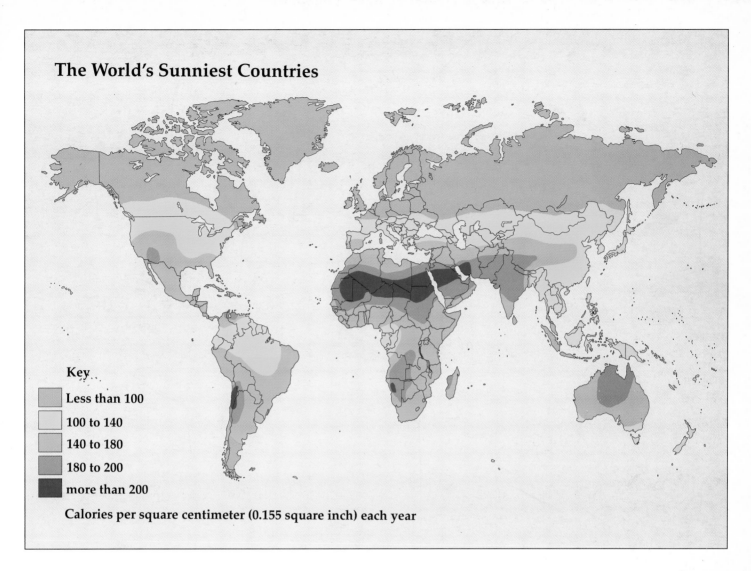

The World's Sunniest Countries

Key

- Less than 100
- 100 to 140
- 140 to 180
- 180 to 200
- more than 200

Calories per square centimeter (0.155 square inch) each year

Solar collectors

The most common method of harnessing solar energy in houses is by using flat-plate collectors. These are glass-topped panels that trap the sun's heat. The trapped heat warms up water in pipes connected to the hot-water tank.

Solar panels work best in hot climates and are widely used in the western United States, the Mediterranean region of Europe, and the Middle East. But they can even extract energy in places where the climate is cloudy and cool.

Solar electricity

A few large solar power plants have been built to produce electricity in the U.S., Australia, Italy, and Japan. Some of these use huge numbers of solar cells. Others use rows of mirrors to reflect sunlight onto a central point, where water is heated to produce steam, which is then used to drive a generator.

▲ A calorie is a measurement of energy. This map shows how much energy from the sun reaches different parts of the world in one year.

Other Energy Sources

The most important of the other renewable energy sources is wind power. People began tapping this energy in sailboats thousands of years ago. Until early in this century windmills were widely used to grind flour and drive pumps and other machinery.

Today in some countries the wind is being harnessed with the wind turbine, the modern version of the windmill. Wind turbines are now collecting energy for many countries.

▼ Wind farms consist of a large number of small turbines. This wind farm is in the Altamont Pass in California.

Wind farms

Places where the wind is used to make electricity are called wind farms. Sometimes a large single turbine is used to generate power. One built on the Hawaiian island of Oahu has rotor blades that are 400 feet across.

In parts of North America and Europe, electricity is now being produced by wind farms that contain large numbers of small turbines arranged in rows.

Most wind turbines have a propeller to pick up the wind. Others use a rotor that spins in an upright position and looks like a giant eggbeater.

Hot rocks

In volcanic regions, hot rocks near the surface provide another useful energy source. When water seeps down to the rocks, it is turned into steam. The steam forces its way back to the surface, where it may emerge as a powerful jet, creating a geyser.

This heat from the earth, or geothermal energy, is already being tapped in several parts of the world, including California, Iceland, Japan, and New Zealand. Natural steam is piped up from underground and used in power plants to drive turbines that generate electricity.

In other countries, experiments are taking place to extract energy from hot rocks that are much deeper underground.

◄ Hot water vapor rises at this geothermal power plant at Wairakei, New Zealand.

▼ This map shows areas of the greatest geothermal activity where energy could be tapped.

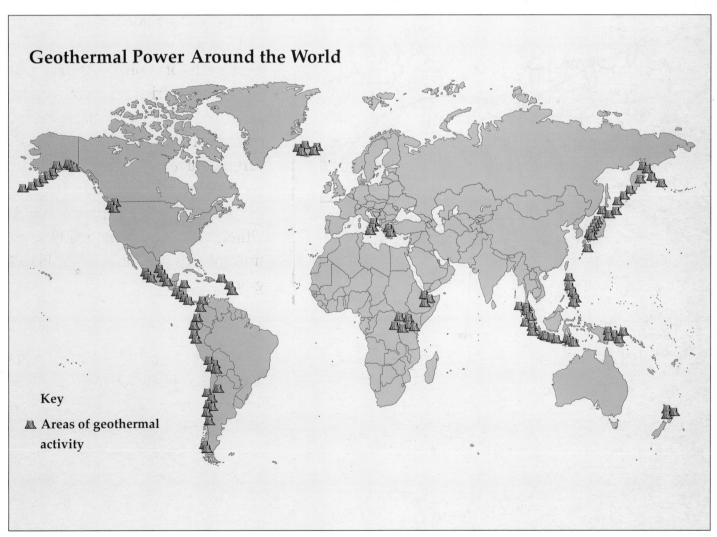

Geothermal Power Around the World

Key
▲ Areas of geothermal activity

Running Out of Fuel

Every year the world is using more and more energy. Most of this energy comes from burning fossil fuels. Supplies of these fuels are limited. They took hundreds of millions of years to form, and once they are gone they cannot be replaced.

No one knows exactly when the fossil fuels will run out. We can make a rough calculation by dividing the amount of known reserves by our current rate of production. On this basis, gas and oil can be expected to last for about another 50 years. Actually, because new oil and gas fields are being found every year, we can expect the fossil fuel supply to last longer.

Other sources of oil

Additionally, different sources of oil are starting to be developed, which could greatly extend our oil reserves. These different sources are oil shales and tar sands. The United States and Canada have vast deposits of these tar-soaked minerals. The largest deposits in the U.S. are the Green River shales in the central states of Utah, Wyoming, and Colorado. In Canada, the main deposits are the Athabasca tar sands in Alberta.

Oil shale and tar sand can be processed into usable oil, but only at a very high cost. So far, only experimental extraction plants are in operation.

▶ Crude oil (in the beaker on the right) can be extracted from this block of oil shale.

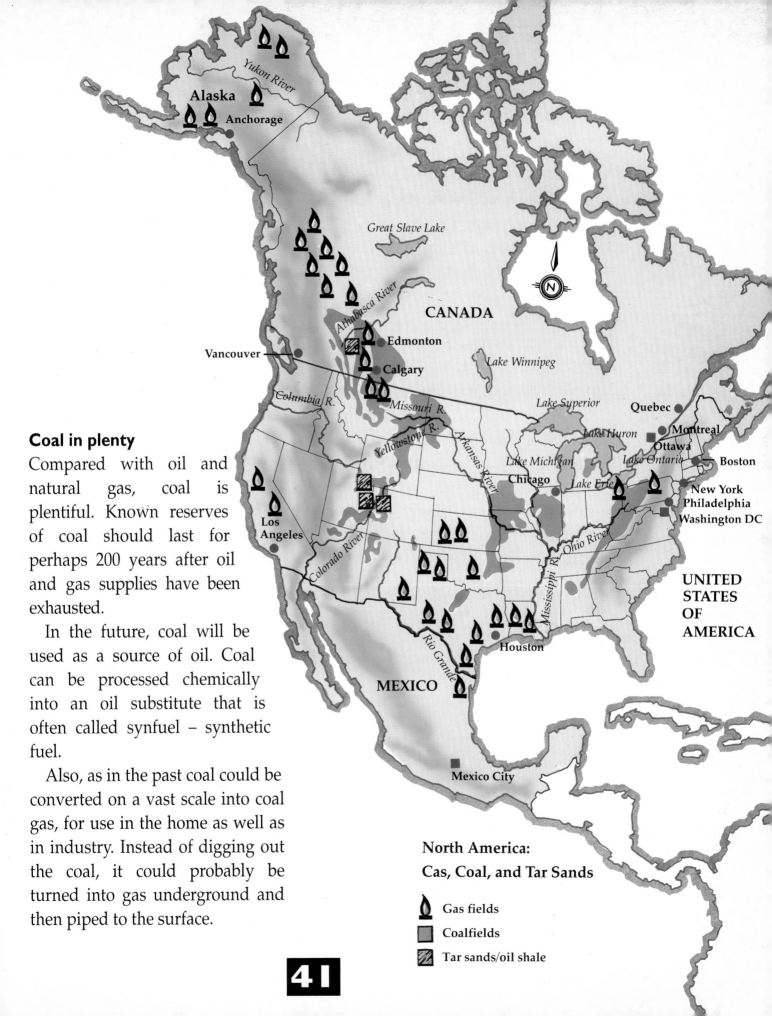

Coal in plenty

Compared with oil and natural gas, coal is plentiful. Known reserves of coal should last for perhaps 200 years after oil and gas supplies have been exhausted.

In the future, coal will be used as a source of oil. Coal can be processed chemically into an oil substitute that is often called synfuel – synthetic fuel.

Also, as in the past coal could be converted on a vast scale into coal gas, for use in the home as well as in industry. Instead of digging out the coal, it could probably be turned into gas underground and then piped to the surface.

North America:

Gas, Coal, and Tar Sands

- Gas fields
- Coalfields
- Tar sands/oil shale

Burning Questions

Coal and oil are both very useful fuels, but they can cause serious pollution when they burn. The majority of power plants burn coal or oil in their furnaces. When these fuels burn, they give off smoke and harmful gases, which escape into the atmosphere. Among these gases are sulfur and nitrogen oxides. Large volumes of nitrogen oxides are also produced by cars.

In the atmosphere, the sulfur and nitrogen oxides combine with water to form droplets of sulfuric and nitric acid. So when it rains, it rains acid. Acid rain attacks trees and vegetation and kills fish and

▼ Many industries produce waste that pollutes the environment, but some of the most harmful pollution comes from burning fossil fuels.

▲ Acid rain destroys vegetation and harms the plants and animals found in lakes and rivers.

other wildlife in rivers and lakes. Acid rain also eats away the stonework on buildings.

The greenhouse effect
Burning fossil fuel produces carbon dioxide gas. This does not pose as much of an immediate threat to the environment as acid

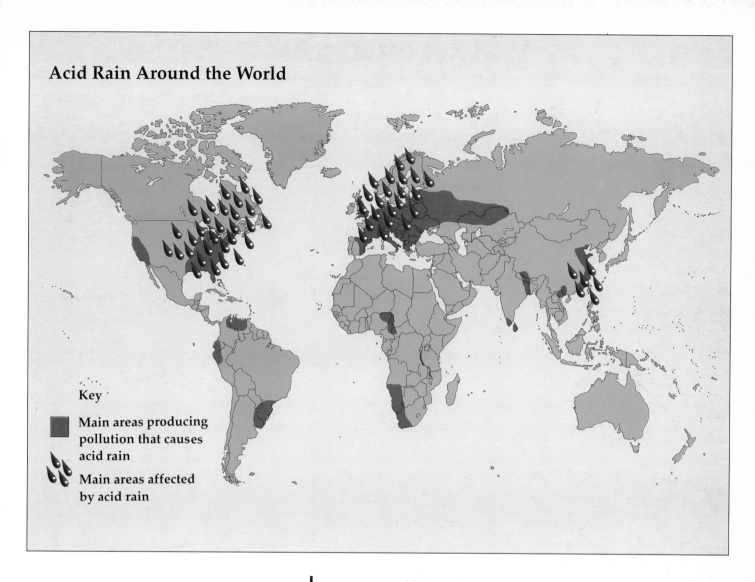

Acid Rain Around the World

Key

Main areas producing pollution that causes acid rain

Main areas affected by acid rain

rain. However, releasing large amounts of carbon dioxide into the atmosphere does pose a serious long-term threat to the environment.

As carbon dioxide builds up in the atmosphere, it traps more of the sun's energy, like a greenhouse does. This "greenhouse effect" already seems to be at work, because world temperatures are gradually rising. This rise in temperatures has become known as "global warming."

If global warming continues, scientists estimate that world temperatures could increase by as much as 40° Fahrenheit by the middle of next century. This would alter climates throughout the world. It would eventually lead to more droughts in some areas, and to extremely heavy rainfall in others. Farming would be particularly hard hit, as farmers would find their crops no longer suitable for the climate.

Power for the Future

The use of fossil fuels causes pollution, and these fuels will run out in the foreseeable future. At the same time, alternative forms of energy from renewable sources are still not producing enough energy to run the world. So the search is on for other sources.

Nuclear power could well be the answer, and our use of it could be increased. But nuclear waste and the possibility of accidents pose a very serious threat to the environment. This is because nuclear reactors and nuclear waste are highly radioactive, and they can remain so for centuries. In large doses, radiation burns the skin and it can kill animals and

▲ The Chernobyl nuclear power plant after the explosion in 1986

people. Small doses of radiation can cause defects in unborn babies.

The dangers of nuclear power were underlined in 1986 when an explosion at the Chernobyl nuclear power plant in the Ukraine released a radioactive cloud that affected countries as far away as England and Norway. Accidents such as this make people worry about using nuclear power.

Fusion not fission

One long-term solution could be nuclear fusion. Fusion is the process that the sun and the stars use to produce energy. During fusion, the nuclei of hydrogen atoms fuse (join together), producing huge amounts of energy. Fusion does not produce radioactive waste, and the fuel it requires can be extracted from water.

▼ This tokomak machine is used in research into nuclear fusion.

◄ These two biodigester units are in use in Mexico, turning animal waste into methane.

Bioenergy

As some scientists look into nuclear fusion, others are looking into ways of producing energy from waste products, such as household garbage and sewage.

When a plant or animal dies, it is attacked by tiny bacteria, which make it decompose (rot). The bacteria are most active in warm, airless conditions. A gas called methane is produced as a by-product of this rotting process. Methane is flammable so it can be used as a source of energy.

Most household garbage is now collected in landfills, enormous pits waiting to be filled up. When each site is full, it is covered with clay and soil. As the garbage rots, it produces methane, which can be piped off for use in industry or the home. In a similar way, human and animal wastes can be collected in a tank (known as a biodigester), which produces methane in the same way.

In Brazil, crops such as sugar cane are grown as a source of bioenergy. The crop is fermented to produce alcohol, which is mixed with gasoline and used as a fuel.

So it may well be that with the further development of nuclear fusion and various forms of bioenergy, our future energy problems will be solved.

Atom The smallest part of a substance that can exist. Atoms are very tiny: one hundred million atoms side by side would measure less than half an inch.

Biodigester A sealed tank in which human or animal wastes or refuse is broken down by bacteria to produce methane gas.

Bioenergy The energy we obtain from the processes of living things, such as bacteria breaking down waste material in a biodigester. This process produces methane gas, which can be used as an energy source.

Chain reaction A rapid reaction like the one that takes place in nuclear fission, in which the splitting of one atom by a neutron releases more neutrons, which cause more atoms to split.

Decompress To remove pressure. The weight of water puts a great deal of pressure on a diver who is deep underwater. To decompress, the diver must rise very slowly to the surface, gradually reducing the pressure of the water. Otherwise, gas bubbles are released in the tissue of the diver's body, often causing paralysis or even death.

Distillation Heating a liquid mixture until the substance required from the mixture turns into a gas. The gas is then collected and cooled, whereupon it condenses (turns back into liquid). The substance required is then separated from the mixture.

Fraction A part of something. In oil refining, a fraction is any one of the various substances obtained by distilling crude oil.

Generator A machine that produces electricity.

Geothermal energy Energy from sources such as hot springs and hot rocks underground. Geothermal means "earth-heat."

Global warming A theory that says the world's climates will change because the atmosphere is getting warmer (see **greenhouse effect**).

Gravity meter An instrument that measures minute variations in the force of gravity at locations where there are certain rock formations. Such variations can act as clues to the presence of rocks known to yield oil.

Greenhouse effect Certain gases in the atmosphere build up and prevent the heat of the sun from escaping. The process is similar to a greenhouse letting the sun's heat in but not letting it out. The greenhouse effect could lead to global warming (see above).

Hydrocarbon A chemical compound that contains hydrogen and carbon. Methane and benzene are hydrocarbons, and gasoline is made up of several different hydrocarbons.

Magnetometer An instrument that measures the strength of a magnetic field.

Naphthol A chemical made from crude oil used to make dyes and antiseptics.

Neutron A tiny particle, smaller than an atom, which is found in the nucleus of almost all atoms. Neutrons are used to bombard atoms so that they split to produce nuclear energy.

Nuclear energy The energy locked in the nucleus of atoms, which is released in nuclear fission.

Nuclear fission The process of splitting the atom to produce nuclear energy.

Nuclear fusion A process that involves joining together, or fusing, the nuclei of atoms to produce energy. This is the process by which energy is produced in the sun and other stars.

Nucleus The central core of an atom.

Petrochemical A chemical that is extracted from petroleum, or crude oil.

Petroleum oil Oil formed in rocks. Also called crude oil.

Radioactive Giving off radiation. Certain chemical elements, including uranium, are radioactive. Radioactive materials are also produced in nuclear reactors. They can be harmful to living things.

Reactor The part of a nuclear power plant where the nuclear chain reaction takes place.

Renewable resource A source of energy that is not reduced when it is used. Coal, for instance, is used up because to turn it into energy it is burned. Hydroelectric power plants, on the other hand, use the energy of running water rather than the water itself, so when the energy is extracted from it, the water is still intact. Water is therefore said to be a renewable resource. Other renewable resources are the winds and the tides, the heat of the sun, and the heat from certain underground rocks.

Turbine A machine with blades like a propeller that spin when water, steam, or gas passes through them. Turbines are used to drive electricity generators. For example, coal or gas is burned to heat water and turn it into steam. The steam is passed at high pressure through a turbine that rotates to drive a generator.

Uranium A metallic element with the properties required for a fuel for nuclear power plants.

Further Reading

Arnold, Guy. *Facts on Water, Wind and Solar Power*. Facts On. New York: Franklin Watts, 1990.

Catherall, Ed. *Exploring Uses of Energy*. Exploring Science. Austin: Raintree Steck-Vaughn, 1990.

Collinson, Alan. *Renewable Energy*. Facing the Future. Austin: Raintree Steck-Vaughn, 1991.

Dunn, Andrew. *Dams*. Structures. New York: Thomson Learning, 1993.

Gosnell, Kelvin. *Nuclear Power Stations*. How It Works. New York: Gloucester Press, 1992.

Kerrod, Robin. *Future Energy and Resources*. Today's World. New York: Gloucester Press, 1990.

Lambert, Mark. *Energy Technology*. Technology in Action. New York: Bookwright Press, 1991.

McKie, Robin. *Energy*. Science Frontiers. New York: Hampstead Press, 1989.

Peacock, Graham. *Electricity*. Resources. New York: Thomson Learning, 1993.

Rickard, Graham. *Oil*. Resources. New York: Thomson Learning, 1993.

Picture Acknowledgments

The publishers would like to thank the following for supplying photographs: J. Allan Cash Library: pages 7 and 39; Hutchison Picture Library: pages 28, 31, and 45; Irish Tourist Board: page 22; Science Photo Library: pages 10 and 40; Frank Spooner Picture Agency: page 44 top; Wayland Picture Library: pages 5, 8 top and bottom, 11, 12, 14 top and bottom, 18, 20 top, 25, 30, 32, 34, 35, 36 top and bottom, 42, and 44 bottom; Zefa: cover, pages 16, 17, 20 bottom, 26, 28 bottom, and 42 top.